Introduction to Olives

Growing Olives in your Garden

Dueep Jyot Singh

Mendon Cottage Books

JD-Biz Publishing

Our books are available at

1. Amazon.com
2. Barnes and Noble
3. Itunes
4. Kobo
5. Smashwords
6. Google Play Books

Table of Contents

Introduction

If you have been reading the ancient holy books, you may find references to the groves of Olives and flourishing olive trees. Olives have long been a part of human social tradition, and they have been cultivated in gardens since time immemorial.

It was believed that olives could not flourish in lands, which were 35 miles away from the sea, because they needed a special type of climate. But that is not really true, because you can grow an olive tree, in a place, where there is plenty of water, where the winters are mild and in areas with Mediterranean climates.

The native olive tree – *Olea europaea* – is considered to be a Mediterranean plant, because after all the ancient Romans and the Greeks used olive leaves as an important symbol – especially of peace. Holding out an olive branch meant PAX and not war. Even the gods blessed the olive tree, and allowed it to flourish on their land, making it prosperous through the sale of olives!

Archaeological surveys in Jordan on sites going back more than 5000 years have found domesticated olives in abundance. So is it a surprise that a garden without an olive tree would be considered to be incomplete even in those ancient days.

Apart from using olives in a diet, olive oil was also used since ancient times for cooking purposes. Apart from that, olive oil was used as a healthy massage oil by Romans, Babylonians, Egyptians, and other ancient civilizations in ancient times.

In ancient Greece, kings as well as victorious athletes were anointed in coronations and the Olympic games with olive oil. The eternal flame of the Olympic game lamp and the oil used to light up the temples was olive oil.

Horace the great Roman poet found inspiration and sustenance in a diet of mallows, endives and olives. The ancients considered this to be one of the perfect foods.

Olives were relatively unknown in the East in these times, because they are basically a Mediterranean native plant. From the northwest of Africa, Iberia, southwestern Mediterranean region, South America, like Chile, Peru, Argentina and South Africa, olives, flourished in lands which had a desert climate.

Olive trees were introduced to California somewhere in the early nineteenth century, where they took very well to the desert area. So if you are living in a land with a dry winter, and a rainy summer, and you have some place where you can allow your olives to grow high, wide and free, this book is going to tell you how you can have an olive grove in your garden!

So how will you recognize the age of an olive tree, apart from the girth and the quality of the wood? The older the tree gets, the more wrinkled, and gnarled the tree trunk is going to be. So a 2000 year old tree is going to be really large, gnarled and still be able to give you a good harvest. The ancient age of the tree can be proved through carbon dating, and apart from being a wonder of nature, you will be able to eat of its fruit and bless the hand that planted it more than two millenniums ago. In Croatia, there is an olive tree, more than 1600 years old, which is still capable of giving 66 pounds of very top-quality olives *every year.*

If you are fortunate enough to visit the well-known Garden of Gethsemane, a number of trees found there are considered to be dating from the days of Jesus and even beyond. Incidentally, Gethsemane means olive press in Hebrew – gat shemanim.

The Greeks massaged their hair and bodies with olive oil to give them a healthy sheen and to stay well groomed.

The slave massaging Messala in Benhur all those millenniums ago, would be using olive oil for his daily massage to keep him in fighting trim for the chariot race. Olive oil is still being used as a massage oil, all over the world.

Growing Olives

Olive trees are very long-lived. So if you plant olives today in your garden, they are going to last for the next millennium! In fact, Pliny wrote about Olive trees and olive groves, more than 2000 years ago, which were more than 1500 years of age in his time. So one could almost believe that these olives were planted when the ancient gods roamed the earth…

These trees are so hardy, that it is almost impossible to kill them off. However, if a plant is destroyed due to severe frost, do not despair. This happened in 1985 in Tuscany, where the climate is mild, and you do not expect a severe winter frost. However, this frost destroyed a number of ancient and productive trees and many farmers thought that they had lost their livelihoods. But they need not have despaired.

The next spring you are going to see new growth springing up from the rootstock. The new shoots are going to spring up as soon as the weather gets warm, and you are going to have fresh new outgrowth.

So this is the reason why the ancient Greeks and the Romans considered olive plants to be immortal plants. It would take a while for these plants to grow again and start bearing fruit, but once they had begun bearing a rich harvest, they would go on and on, spreading their bounty and shade upon the land.

Olive trees like soil, which is full of calcium. That is why they are going to grow really well on crags and slopes, made up of limestone rich mountains and hills – and if these happen to be in coastal areas, so much the better. However, you can grow them in any sort of soil, as long as it is, well-drained. I would not suggest a too rich soil, because that is more prone to disease. The oil content is also going to be poorer, and the quality is not going to be what you expect, from a too rich over fertilized soil.

Imagine an olive tree growing, on the top of the mountain, and in a desert area. You are rarely going to find too much of organic matter here, except from natural soil particles in the mountains, brought down by the rains, and collecting there due to the action of the weather or through erosion. It is only a very hardy plant, which can manage to grow and survive under such circumstances.

These plants enjoy hot weather. That is why the olives of Greece have been well-known in the ancient world. These trees were normally planted in sunny areas, and they speak about Socrates , preaching his philosophy to the younger Athenian generation in an olive grove. As a preacher is never honored in his own country, he was condemned to be put to death with poison hemlock. Centuries later Pliny talked about Socrates' Grove, with its ancient trees.

Make sure the temperature should not go down below -10°C, which is 14°F. Even a hardy tree cannot survive this low temperature. Dry climates and even drought conditions do not bother them much. That is because they have a really extensive and deep rooted root system.

Like I said before, olives are slow-growing plants. However, because of their magnificent girth, you have to make sure that they have plenty of available and elbow space in which to grow. They have been plants known, which have measured 33 feet in girth. That means ten of us normal sized beings can sit under the shade of this tree and enjoy a picnic.

The height of a normal olive tree is going to be up to 49 feet in its wild stage. However, you can keep the height under control by pruning it. Apart from the fruit, the wood is also considered to be very precious, especially for woodcraft and woodworking. That is because it is brownish green in color and has an attractive, darkly tinted vein running through it. The wood is also fire resistant.

Olive trees can either be self-fertile, – the Pendolino varieties but if you need a large crop, you would need pollenizers, which are the Maurino and the Leccino varieties. So if you want a really rich harvest in your olive tree Grove, make sure that you have plenty of Pendolino trees growing in it.

Olive Propagation

You can either grow olives from seed, or you can propagate the trees from layers and cuttings. If you have olive seeds ready at hand, you can soften up the oily pericarp by allowing it to rot for a little while. This is done by soaking it in slightly hot water or in a very mild alkaline solution and then putting it out in the air in order to rot. This is going to facilitate seed germination.

Sowing by the seeds is done in October/November. If you do not want to put the seeds beforehand, in an alkaline solution, you can remove the tip with a sharp pin to allow the entry of moisture in the seed. Make sure that the seed beds are watered frequently so that they have plenty of moisture.

Seedlings are going to attain graft-able size, when they are about eighteen months old.

Also, if you are using root cuttings, you can just plant them in well-prepared and rich soil, and the tree is going to germinate./Root and throw suckers. You can find plenty of these suckers growing from stumps, after the olive trees have been cut down. However, any seedling yield, which is germinated from a seed or from a sucker is going to be poor, that is why since ancient times, olive plants have always been grafted or budded onto other trees.

That is because an olive seed may lie dormant for about a year, before it decides to germinate olive seeds have a very hard shell, which has to be soft and, before germination. So if you are trying to raise plants from seeds, sow them individually in pots, write down the date and hope for the best.

Alternatively, you can take a number of branches of different thicknesses. Cut them into 1 m lengths. Plant them deeply into well manured soil. These are going to vegetate rapidly.

Other traditional methods of getting olives ready for propagation is by taking shorter pieces of healthy branch wood, and laying them horizontally in trenches. Cover them with the little bit of soil. They are going to give shoots.

In ancient Greece a branch from a cultivated tree was grafted to a wild olive tree. In many parts of Italy, small buds, which grow on stems are cut very carefully and then planted in rich soil. They are going to give you a really healthy and vigorous olive plant shoot. These buds sowings are normally done in March and April, depending on the area in which you are growing the plant.

Take the cuttings in summer, and make sure that they are of semi-hardwood or terminal cuttings. Remove the leaves from the lower half portion of the cuttings. You may want to prepare the soil, beforehand, with plenty of organic material. Plant the cuttings there, until the roots start to grow.

Olives are evergreen plants. They need a little bit of chilling, for fruiting purposes. This is common in temperate region, fruit plants, when temperatures fall down at night. The wilder varieties of olives *O.oleaster*

are not cultivated, because being a wild species, it is much better to use these trees for grafting purposes. Also, the fruit of these olives are inedible and the tree is spiny.

The one which you are going to cultivate in your garden, apart from the Pendolino variety is going to be the O. *europea* variety *sativa*. This is going to be the cultivated oil yielding form, with lots of foliage, and a good harvest of fruits.

An olive is going to grow well in a warm and temperate to subtropical regions, where the temperature ranges between 7 – 35°C. If you are trying to grow olives at an altitude, make sure that the height is just 750 – 1450 m above sea level. Higher than that, your tree is not going to flourish.

Growing olive trees is done best in areas where the rainfall is well distributed. If the winter rain is inadequate, or there is a delay in it, the new vegetative growth is going to be delayed. This is going to create a significant reduction in the growth and differentiation of the flower bud. In the same manner, if there is a continuous dry and hot summer spell, along with a serious water shortage, you are not going to get a good flower or fruit growth.

The rest period is broken with chilling, which is going to promote the growth of fruit and a good harvest. The cold winds of autumn is not beneficial, because then you are not going to get mature fruit and thus good quality oil content. In the same way, if you area is prone to hailstorms, sorry, you cannot grow olives, there.

Last year, we were astonished to see *hailstorms* in our area, in the month of June. Three days previously, the temperature was 45°C in the shade. Apart from the weirdness quotient, – who could believe such an unbelievable thing, especially in the summer,-when even the meanest intellect could understand that there was some weather experimentation going on somewhere, underground, in some lab because one never expects hailstorms in desert areas and never ever in summer. There was no question of a hailstorm in this particular area, even in the winters, and even when the temperature went below -5°C.

But the sad thing is that this unusual freak of weather destroyed all the twenty olive trees being grown in an experimental agro research station in our area. One of my research professor friends was discouraged enough to say that she was definitely not going to start growing trees and plants, which were normally not natives of our area, if they were to be regularly subjected to unusual freak weather sent to us courtesy some barking mad scientists somewhere. She was in a bad temper! But then, so would I be.

This was also unbelievable and no sane person- read project research director – would believe cold icy hailstorms in June as an acceptable explanation for the death of those trees. Would you?

Unfortunately, weather experimentation is being done under the close supervision of a number of ruthless Enterprises with unlimited funding in many parts of the world, targeting other parts of the world just to see the fun. But my dream of eating fresh olives – the trees were just getting ready to fruit – has all gone to rack and ruin, because of a hailstorm in June!

Popular Varieties

Pendolino varieties are capable of giving you about 30 pounds per tree. Mission, Picholine, Frontoio and Coratina are capable of giving up to 20 pounds per tree. If you are growing olives in a low altitude area, you can grow the Canino, Leccino and Moriolo variety.

I was just talking with one of my friends, about olive varieties, and I started getting amused at the varieties – Canino reminded me of dogs and Cornicobra reminded me of a loony serpent. When he had stopped guffawing, he said that according to him, many of the variety names were rather logical, and that the person who had named these varieties made sure that they would be remembered. So they would!

But then I being rather a cynic remember Barbara Cartland's silly vapid heroines with equally stupid names made up of a couple of consonants and a couple of vowels. For example, a heroine named Ola decides to disguise herself and change her name. Her two choices of suitable names are Holeola and Relola. I ask you. Only a Barbara Cartland could think these names attractive or believable.

So how can an olive tree be majestic, if it knows that it belongs to the Cornicobra or Grosseune (The Fat One) variety? Nevertheless, these varieties give you anywhere between 15 – 25 pounds of fruit per tree. Ascolano is going to give you olives best for pickling, but just about 12 pounds – 15 pounds per year. Hats off to the ancient sixty-six pounder per year, referred to somewhere up above.

Sevillano is the variety grown in Spain, and it ranks third in California. This tree is not so strong growing as *Manzanillo*. The fruit is much larger, but it is lower in oil content – 12 – 18%. It is also more firm in texture.

Other popular varieties growing all over the world are *Barouni* and *Chemlali* in Tunisia, *Nevadillo Blanco* and *N. Negro, Cornicabra, Arbequin, Verdal* and *Negral.* In Italy, you are going to get *Rotendella, Olivetta, Ogliarola, Biancolilla*, and *Moraiola.*

A large number of olive varieties are grown in Greece because of its considerable diversity of climate and soil. The humid maritime temperature and dry continental air as well as frost free coastal districts to higher frosty areas are all capable of producing olive trees, especially trees with greater resistance to low temperatures like plants of the *Mastoides Mina* variety.

The olives grown in France are suitable only for pickling or for oil. As the olive plant is a hardy one, it can grow in most countries where sources of water are low, especially in northern Africa. Apart from these olive trees grow well in Western Asia, in China and in Japan.

Much of the most extensive cultivation of olives now is in Spain, which grows about 37% of the world's olive crop. After that comes, Italy, Greece, Portugal and Tunisia .

The olive seeds which were brought to California to Mexico by Franciscan priests were planted for the first time in San Diego from these seedlings cuttings were sent to other missions. These plans are very vigorous and sometimes the trees become too tall for economic harvesting!

Table and Mill Olives

There are two well-defined classes of fruit utilization. Some of these olives are going to be table olives. The others are going to be mill olives. The mill olives are going to have more oil and lower content of sugar and water when compared to the olives grown for table use. Cross pollinated olive trees are going to give you a better yield of fruit.

In many Mediterranean areas, planting of olives is normally done in July/August. In some places it is also done in winter, especially December/January, if there are plenty of good irrigation facilities easily available. The seedlings spacing is going to be anywhere between 6 – 8 m on either way depending on the type of the soil and the cultivars.

Traditionally, olive growers dug up pits of one cubic meter size, one month prior to the planting. This was then filled up with topsoil, manure mixture, organic mixture, and any other nutrients, which could be assimilated within one month after making the soil really rich. If you are planting a graft, the graft union should be kept 15 cm above the ground level. This is to avoid collar rot.

The trees should be planted 5 cm deeper than they were in the nursery. In dry and sandy soils, you will need to plant them even deeper, because it will be easier for their root system to go hunting for water if the plant has been planted quite deep in the initial stages.

Soil Conditions

The best soil for olives is a silt clay soil. Soil to the depth of one – 2 m is quite suitable for this plant. The subsoil is going to be more important because it is going to affect the development of a deep-rooted root system. It is not going to grow well on a wet soil, because that means the waterlogging prevents proper root growth.

The soil pH of 6.5 – 7.5 is best for olives. If the soil is too alkaline, with a pH of 8.5 or more, the productivity and the growth is going to be affected.

Soil Moisture

It is necessary to maintain proper levels of soil moisture, during the growing season. This is going to ensure adequate tree growth and a higher yield of fruit. This is achieved by providing 1000 mm of water during March to September.

Olive trees need irrigation 30 days, prior to the expected flowering period. This is going to promote satisfactory development of the flower buds. This is also going to reduce the flower and fruit drop. Another irrigation is also going to be provided 15 days after the peak flowering. This is to improve the fruit set. The last irrigation is 30 days after fruit set. This is going to encourage the development of fruits. It is also going to reduce the summer drop of the fruit.

Pruning

Your olive trees are going to need regular pruning, in order to live long and flourish. Lots of foliage is good enough, but without pruning, how are you going to get a really good olive harvest year after year after year?

In France, especially in Provence, this strict pruning is done by preserving the previous year's shoot, which have borne flowers. The tree is kept at a low height, so that the fruit can be gathered easily. Fertilizer, when placed in the soil is placed between the trees, and not directly around the roots. Even though a crop can be enormous, you cannot get a really good crop, two times running, from the same old plant. That is why farmers in France and Italy are happy with the huge crop, they obtain every fifth – seventh season.

Traditionally bearing trees are not pruned, except for the removal of dead and interfering branches. The old shoots and the weak are thinned out so as to keep the trees in a strong, healthy and vigorously growing condition.

If the plant is left unpruned, it is going to become too tall and unmanageable. That is why, you need to cut away the upright shoots, which are growing away strongly from the center of the tree.This way, the tree is going to grow in girth but it is not going to grow so much in height.

Traditionally olive trees are generally trained and pruned in such a manner that they have a global and hemispherical shape. The tree should be staked out to allow it to stand firmly without rubbing against the support stake. Get rid of the undesirable and unnecessary suckers. In some cases, you may leave some suckers on, which do not oppose the framework of the tree.

As the trees get older most of the main scaffold branches are going to be pruned so that new vigorous growth is carried out. This new growth is going to begin fruiting after 2 years.

Harvesting of the Fruit

All of these are olive varieties…

Olives are harvested when their deep green color begins to change to a lighter and straw yellow color. Therefore, this is the time when you have to look out for the fruit becoming too soft at that stage. This normally happens in some varieties. So make sure that you harvest the fruit, before they reach the soft stage.

You can allow the firm fleshed varieties to stay on the branches until you see the tinge of purple coloration on their skins. The right time for harvesting is going to be learned through experience. So if you are the 1st time harvester, ask the help of an experienced olive fruit grower to tell the right time and season for harvest. That is because if the fruits are harvested too soon, they are going to lose their flavor, as well as their texture.

Handling of the olives has to be done carefully, because they are very easily bruised.

A heavy crop of olives on the trees is going to reduce size of the fruit. On most large fruited varieties used for pickling and canning and on some small fruited varieties which are grown for oil, a heavy crop is going to reduce the size of the crop. It may also prevent fruiting in the succeeding year.

This alternate bearing of root is not always associated with the failure of the tree to blossom in the off year. It is more because of the reduced ability of flowers to set fruit following a heavy crop.

Alternating however, is going to be less pronounced on trees where the soil has plenty of water and lots of nutrient. You may want to add extra nitrogen in the spring when a new crop is being set. This is going to cause enough leafy growth surface, causing more fruit to be set in the succeeding year.

Olives for Taste

Olives have a natural and unpalatable bitterness, most of which has to be removed before they can be enjoyed with pleasure. I remember the 1st episode of *The Persuaders* when the 2 main characters, Tony Curtis and Roger Moore, have a little bit of an argument about the number of olives which need to be put in a "Tree Climber."

Tony is busy giving gratuitous advice to the bartender and asking him to put two olives in Roger Moore's – who is a complete stranger to him – drink.

"Lord Brett Sinclair" definitely does not want this advice because he does not want "two olives, bumping against each other in his drink!" So they settle matters by getting into an argument -with fisticuffs- destroying the whole bar in the process!

Later on in the episode, when the 2 men are *finally* introduced to each other, they still cannot resist a 1 olive/2 olives dialogue thus setting the stage for future arguments based on individual taste and stubbornness.

Well, the idea of an olive in a drink is definitely a fashion statement. Especially James Bond, who liked his Vodka Martini with an olive. The olive fruit is a drupe and bitter in taste. Olives are an acquired taste. That is why they need to be treated beforehand, before they can be eaten in fashionable quantities, without you puckering up your mouth.

This is normally done by soaking the fruits in a solution of caustic soda. The usual strength of this caustic soda lye is between $1.25 - 2.00\%$. Green olives are kept completely submerged in this lye because exposure to the air is going to darken the color of the olive and turn it a darker shade.

So it does not matter whether you are eating your olives pickled or seasoned in your drinks, which are shaken not stirred. Olives are going to be added to bump on the surface, take it or leave it.

Olives are also an essential part of cuisine, all over the world. Not only are they an important source of cooking oil, but imagine making a salad oil without olive oil. In the same manner, imagine hors d'oeuvres without olives before you spring the main course upon your unsuspecting guests. These olives are going to provide a contrast in color, flavor and texture to the other ingredients of the hors d'oeuvres or salads.

I remember listening to one of my father's favorite stories about a father dipping into a bowl of olives and eating them with relish. His kid appeared in the vicinity and began eating olives too. After both of them had three olives each, the kid began to howl. The surprised father asked him the reason why he was crying and the kid answered that his father was getting all the good ones!

Well, the kid is right. Like I said, Eating olives is an acquired taste and I would not have more than two small slices of olives – just for taste – on my homemade pizza with greens, cheese, chicken, tomatoes, onions, mayonnaise, and anything else in the fridge.

Extracting Olive Oil

There are many traditional ways of extracting olive oil and nowadays mechanical processes are much in use. In one process, the fruit is separated from leaves and other extra plant parts and washed. They are then crushed by roller so adjusted as to break very few seeds, if any.

Olive fruit being ground.

This is then collected in strong cloths, and then subjected to a pressure of 1000 pounds so that most of the juice and some of the oil is extracted. This is called a *pomace.*

This pomace is then crushed again in a bowl under heavy rollers and exposed to considerably greater pressure. This expressed material is then placed in a second tank and the oil, which rises to the top is removed. It is then washed by being sprayed into warm water or having warm water sprayed into it to remove the bitter substance that has come from the fruit with it.

This oil is then going to be placed again in settling tanks for 10 days so that the solid particles and some of the heaviest oils, sink down to the bottom. These are now drawn off from the bottom. This oil if used for food is going to be filtered, aged in a tank and filtered again. People prefer oils refined to tastelessness in a large number of markets, but a little bit of bitter taste, which comes with less filtering is going to leave a richer flavor.

The remaining cold pomace may be pressed for a third time, strongly enough to extract seed oil, as well as some of the remaining pulp oil. This is going to contain more of the high melting point oils, as well as the seed oil. This is usually not mixed up with that oil obtained from earlier pressings. The oil still remaining in the press cake can be extracted with chemical solvents and is normally used for making soaps and beauty products.

In places where it is not always easy to extract oil as fast as it can be harvested, the fruit is either left on the trees, until it can be used, or it is harvested and stored.

If you are storing the fruit, remember not to leave it too long in bins or sacks. This long storage is going to cause rotting. It is also going to cause a deterioration in the quality of the oil.

In olden times olives were stored in a 4% – 6% sodium chloride solution, or in dripping water for 60 days or longer. This prevented spoilage. For storage longer than 60 days, the temperature should be around 40°F or a little lower.

The ultra-refined olive oil that you get in the market today has been subjected to so many refining processes that most of its flavor and taste has been removed. It is good only for putting on salads. Look for places where you can get real olive oil produced by local growers, especially in the Mediterranean regions, Greece and Italy.

Conclusion

This book has given you plenty of information about the origin and history of olives, as well as how you can grow it as a profitable plant.

Here are some interesting URLs which are going to tell you more about olives and their uses.

I found this particular URL quite fascinating and informative –

http://anrcatalog.ucdavis.edu/pdf/8267.pdf

This is also interesting for general knowledge.

http://www.chatelaine.com/health/diet/five-health-benefits-of-olives-and-olive-oil-plus-a-zesty-tapenade-recipe/

http://www.naturalblaze.com/2013/10/10-reasons-you-should-be-eating-olives.html

This URL by John Summerley is also very informative, especially when he talks about not buying olives in cans. Being a natural food promoter myself, I do not advise anything which is bottled or canned, by companies unless you are doing the bottling and canning yourself.

So take full advantage of the health benefits of olives and Live Long and Prosper!

Author Bio

Dueep Jyot Singh is a Management and IT Professional who managed to gather Postgraduate qualifications in Management and English and Degrees in Science, French and Education while pursuing different enjoyable career options like being an hospital administrator, IT,SEO and HRD Database Manager/ trainer, movie , radio and TV scriptwriter, theatre artiste and public speaker, lecturer in French, Marketing and Advertising, ex-Editor of Hearts On Fire (now known as Solstice) Books Missouri USA, advice columnist and cartoonist, publisher and Aviation School trainer, ex-moderator on Medico.in, banker, student councilor ,travelogue writer … among other things!

One fine morning, she decided that she had enough of killing herself by Degrees and went back to her first love—writing. It's more enjoyable! She already has 48 published academic and 14 fiction- in- different- genre books under her belt.

When she is not designing websites or making Graphic design illustrations for clients , she is browsing through old bookshops hunting for treasures, of which she has an enviable collection – including R.L. Stevenson, O.Henry, Dornford Yates, Maurice Walsh, De Maupassant, Victor Hugo, Sapper, C.N. Williamson, "Bartimeus" and the crown of her collection- Dickens "The Old Curiosity Shop," and "Martin Chuzzlewit" and so on… Just call her "Renaissance Woman") - collecting herbal remedies, acting like Universal Helping Hand/Agony Aunt, or escaping to her dear mountains for a bit of exploring, collecting herbs and plants and trekking.

Check out some of the other JD-Biz Publishing books

Gardening Series on Amazon

Health Learning Series

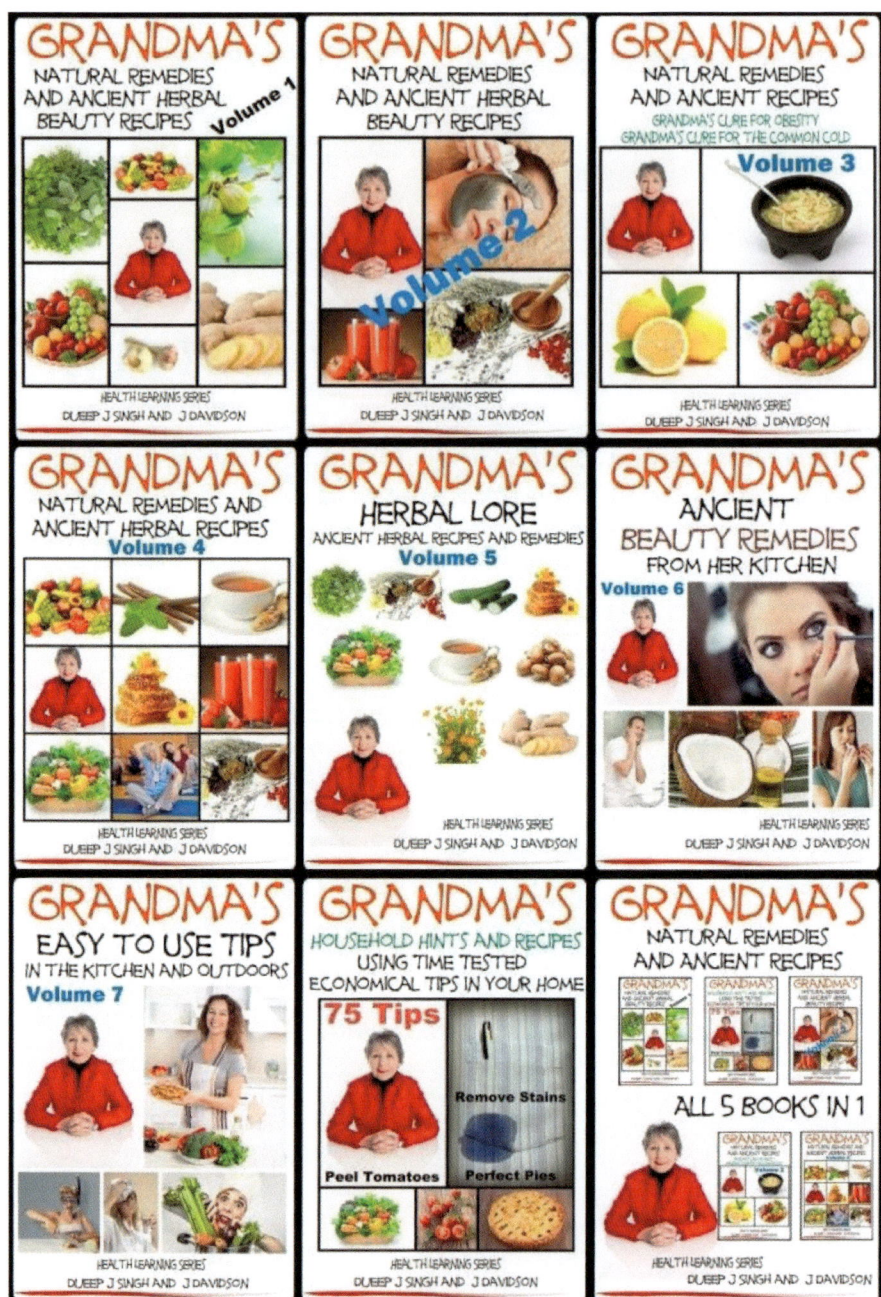

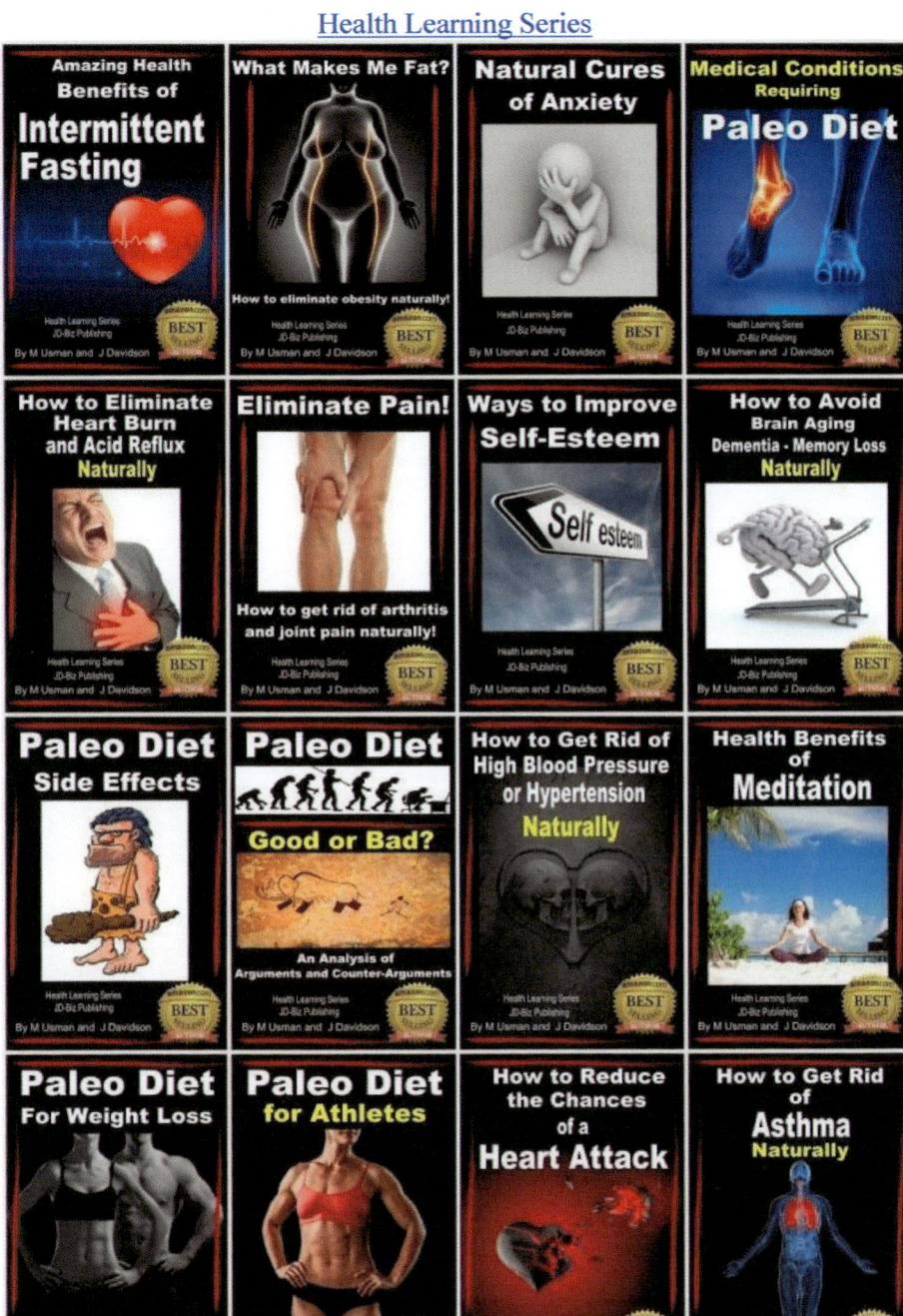

Amazing Animal Book Series

Learn To Draw Series

How to Build and Plan Books

Entrepreneur Book Series

Our books are available at

1. Amazon.com

2. Barnes and Noble

3. Itunes

4. Kobo

5. Smashwords

6. Google Play Books

Publisher

JD-Biz Corp

P O Box 374

Mendon, Utah 84325

http://www.jd-biz.com/

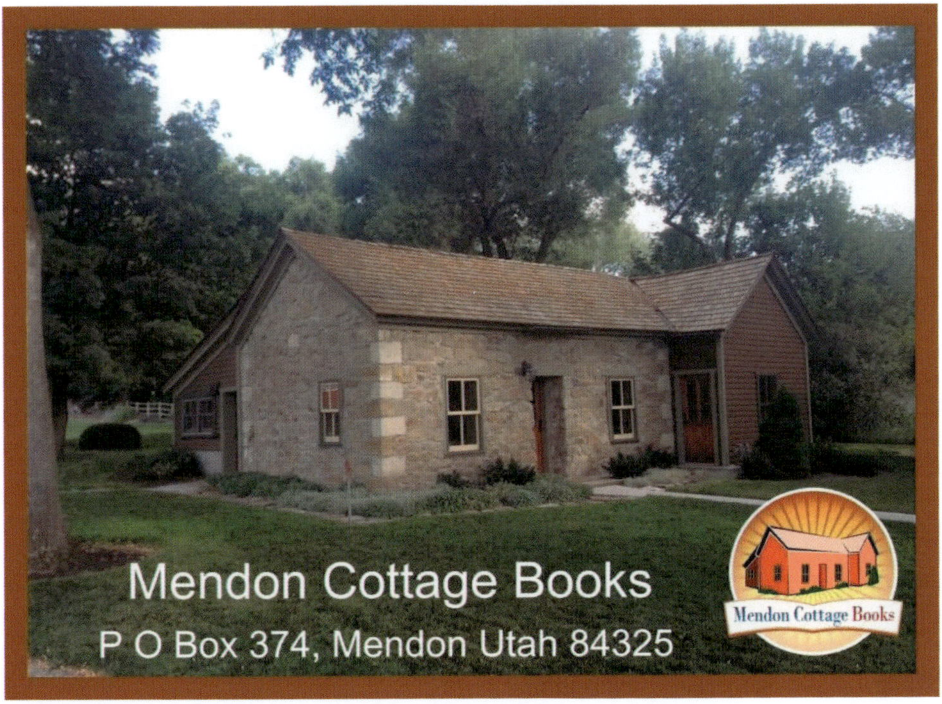

Mendon Cottage Books

P O Box 374, Mendon Utah 84325

Printed in Great Britain
by Amazon